CREEPY CRAWLIES

Buzz off, Flies!

Rachel Eagen

Crabtree Publishing Company

www.crabtreebooks.com

Developed and produced by Plan B Book Packagers

Author:
Rachel Eagen

Editorial director:
Ellen Rodger

Art director:
Rosie Gowsell-Pattison

Logo design:
Margaret Amy Salter

Editor:
Molly Aloian

Proofreader:
Crystal Sikkens

Project manager:
Kathy Middleton

Production coordinator & prepress technician:
Katherine Berti

Photographs:
National Institutes of Health: p. 10 (top)
Photos.com: cover, logo
Shutterstock: cover, p. 1–2; 6493866629: p. 28 (bottom);
Alexey Antipov: p. 26 (left); Katrina Brown: p. 25 (top);
Norman Chan: p. 25 (bottom); Arindam Das: p. 16 (top);
Digital Media Pro: p. 3, 12; Melissa Dockstader: p. 6 (top);
Draconus: p. 13 (bottom); EJ white: p. 6 (bottom);
Feverpitch: p. 24; Four Oaks: p. 22 (top); Cindy Haggerty:
p. 20; Patricia Hofmeester: p. 9 (bottom); Gasa: p. 17;
Nick Gorelov: p. 19 (top); Péter Gudella: p. 11 (bottom);
Eric Isselée: p. 7 (bottom); Liew Weng Keong: p. 14;
Robert Kneschke: p. 27 (bottom); Konkolas: p. 10 (bottom);
Harm Kruyshaar: p. 5 (top); Lush: p. 19 (top); Roger
De Marfa: p. 11 (top); Alon Othnay: p. 22 (bottom);
Pakhnyushcha: p. 7 (top); Phenomania: p. 29 (top);
pz Axe: p. 26 (right); Javier Rejon: p. 4; Rieke Photos:
p. 21 (top); Jane Rix: p. 23; Jose Ignacio Soto: p. 8;
Subbotina Anna: p. 13 (top), 28 (top), 29 (middle);
Svic: p. 21 (bottom); Nikita Tiunov: p. 18; Tomashko:
p. 5 (bottom); Rick Whitacre: p. 29 (bottom);
Zenphotography: p. 16 (bottom)

Library and Archives Canada Cataloguing in Publication

Eagen, Rachel, 1979-
    Buzz off, flies! / Rachel Eagen.

(Creepy crawlies)
Includes index.
ISBN 978-0-7787-2499-5 (bound).--ISBN 978-0-7787-2506-0 (pbk.)

    1. Flies--Juvenile literature. 2. Flies as carriers of disease--Juvenile literature. I. Title. II. Series: Creepy crawlies (St. Catharines, Ont)

QL533.2.E23 2010   j595.77   C2010-901755-2

Library of Congress Cataloging-in-Publication Data

Eagen, Rachel.
Buzz off, flies! / Rachel Eagen.
    p. cm. -- (Creepy crawlies)
Includes index.
ISBN 978-0-7787-2499-5 (reinforced lib. bdg. : alk. paper)
-- ISBN 978-0-7787-2506-0 (pbk. : alk. paper)
1. Flies as carriers of disease--Juvenile literature. 2. Flies--Juvenile literature.
I. Title. II. Series.

RA641.F6E24 2011
614.4'322--dc22
                                    2010009550

Crabtree Publishing Company

www.crabtreebooks.com   1-800-387-7650
Printed in China/072010/AP20100226

Published in Canada
Crabtree Publishing
616 Welland Ave.
St. Catharines, Ontario
L2M 5V6

Published in the United States
Crabtree Publishing
PMB 59051
350 Fifth Avenue, 59th Floor
New York, New York 10118

Published in the United Kingdom
Crabtree Publishing
Maritime House
Basin Road North, Hove
BN41 1WR

Published in Australia
Crabtree Publishing
386 Mt. Alexander Rd.
Ascot Vale (Melbourne)
VIC 3032

Contents

Buzz Off!

What is that annoying whine? How did those disgusting worms get into the dog's dish? What made those horrible bites that itch like crazy? The answer to these creepy questions is FLIES, one of the world's most important insects.

They're Everywhere!

Flies live wherever we do. It's creepy but true! Their tiny size allows them to eat, breed, and **defecate** in the smallest nooks and crannies. Flies are not picky eaters. All they need to survive is a little garbage and a warm place to rest their wings and lay their eggs. Insect experts, known as **entomologists**, have identified about 120,000 **species**, or groups, of flies, but there are thought to be twice as many that have yet to be named. Flies can be found buzzing around garbage, food, dead animals, or pet **feces** on every continent.

Flies have poor reputations, often due to their bad table manners, that include landing on dog feces, then flying to your dinner table.

Friend or Foe?

Flies are germ spreaders and disease carriers. They feed on dog feces before attacking picnics. They infect humans with diseases, such as **typhoid**. For all of their faults, flies play an important role in the world. They help break down **decaying** waste. Without flies, the planet would turn into an enormous trash dump! Flies are also important pollinators, which means they help **fertilize** flowers and other plants. It is a good thing, too, because whether we like it or not, flies are here to stay.

Flies belong to a large order of insects called *Diptera*, which is a Latin word that can be broken down into two other words. Di means two, and ptera means wings. In other words, flies have one pair of wings.

CRAWLY FACT

True Fly Shoo Fly

Not all flies are real flies. As confusing as that sounds, it is pretty simple. Only true flies belong to the *Diptera* order, which means they have one pair of wings, and one set of halteres, the knobby structures that sit behind the wings. There are many winged insects that have fly-like names, but they are fakes because they have at least two pairs of wings. Gnats, mosquitoes, midges, and houseflies are true flies. Dragonflies, mayflies, and butterflies are not.

Dragonflies are not true flies.

Flies are known for having some pretty disgusting habits. For starters, their diet is not exactly appetizing. They use a long, hollow mouthpart called a proboscis to suck up liquid foods, which can include rotten fruit, feces, sweat, and pus from open sores.

Germ Carriers

A single fly carries about one million germs on its body. Just one hairy foot is covered in thousands of **bacteria** that can be spread to animals and humans. Flies swarm garbage cans, dipping their legs in rotten meat and other disgusting things. They then land on our food, sprinkling it with bacteria before they take off. Flies spread many illnesses this way. True flies that bite can also infect humans with deadly diseases.

When flies land on food, they bring microscopic bits of food from their last meal with them. Bits of dog feces cling to their legs and are spread to that yummy pie cooling on the windowsill.

Hosting a Party...

Some true flies are **parasites**, which means they live on hosts, or other animals. Human botflies lay their eggs on mosquitoes. When the mosquito bites a human, it leaves an egg inside the bite, where it hatches into a **maggot**. The maggot feeds on the human's flesh, making a large, painful sore on the surface of the skin. When the maggot grows to about one inch (2.5 cm) in length, it drops out of its host, and tunnels into the ground, where it becomes an adult fly.

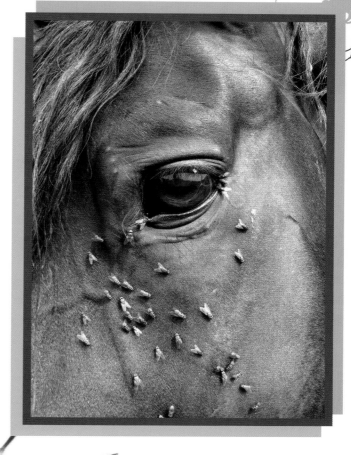

Flies leave a trail of sticky saliva on everything they touch.

Horses use their tails to swat flies off of their bodies. They also twitch their muscles to flick annoying flies away from areas they can't reach with their tails.

THAT'S CREEPY

River Blindness

In the warm regions of Africa and Central America, black flies carry a disease called river blindness. The disease is caused by worms that live in the flies' saliva. When the flies bite a human, they leave their eggs, which can become very itchy and uncomfortable when they hatch. If the maggots get into the eyes, they can cause blindness.

Ancient Annoyance

Flies have swarmed the Earth for over 200 million years. Flies have evolved since then, **adapting** to new environments as the world around them changed. It is because of their ability to adapt that there are so many species of flies today.

Trapped by Time

Millions of years ago, sap oozed from cracks in trees. The sweet smell attracted flies and other insects, which became trapped in the sticky syrup. Over time, the sap hardened into a rock-hard substance called **amber**. Samples of insects trapped in ancient amber have allowed scientists to learn more about ancient insects. For example, an amber sample found in New Jersey in 1996 included 100 different species of insects and plants. One of these insects was the world's oldest mosquito, which was over 90 million years old.

Little Soldiers

The ancient Egyptians had a special relationship with flies. They knew that flies carried germs, so they had fly whisks to brush them away. The Egyptians also believed that flies were courageous because they attacked animals that were much bigger than them, such as goats and cows. For this reason, Egyptian soldiers who were courageous on the battlefield were rewarded with fly necklaces fashioned from gold and silver.

The ancient Egyptians lined their eyes with kohl, a lead-based cosmetic that flies hated. This kept flies from buzzing around their eyes, preventing a nasty infection called conjunctivitis, or pink eye.

True Survivors

Flies followed people as they conquered new territories and built settlements. Maggots that lived in food on ships hatched and found new homes in the **New World**. In those days, people bathed and washed their clothes infrequently, which meant that flies laid eggs on people's bodies, especially in their armpits, and in the pockets of their clothes. Farm animals also crawled with parasitic flies.

Flies at War

Over a hundred years ago, doctors understood that flies could be used to help people. During the **American Civil War** (1861–1865), blowfly maggots were attached to soldiers' infected wounds, where they feasted on the infected flesh. The crawling, chewing maggots created an extremely uncomfortable sensation, but the suffering was necessary. Without the help of powerful medicines, infected wounds could easily lead to the **amputation** of an arm or leg. These flesh-eating flies got rid of dead tissue and helped save the limbs of many wounded soldiers.

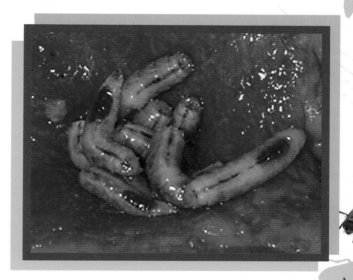

Maggots eat dead tissue surrounding a wound.

Flies love an easy meal and livestock are a favorite target because it is hard for them to brush flies away.

Fly Family

There are about 120,000 different species of flies known today, but it is thought that there are still another 120,000 that have yet to be identified. Flies evolved over millions of years and developed new behaviors and body structures that would allow them to survive in changing environments. With so much adapting, scientists today know that we have missed out on studying hundreds, if not thousands of species of flies that used to buzz around the planet. Many have since become extinct.

Fly Class

Today, animals are identified and named according to a system of classification that has been used for almost 300 years. The man who created this system is Carl Linnaeus, a Swedish scientist who loved nature and wanted to learn everything he could about it. In 1738, Linnaeus published a book called *Systema Naturae*, in which he named and described many different species of plants. In the 1740s, he began classifying animals, too. His system of naming and describing living things is now known as **taxonomy**.

Carl Linnaeus developed a system of classification for plants and animals. The system is still used today, although it has been updated to be more scientifically accurate.

In the Kingdom

So how did Linnaeus' system of classification work? First, he grouped all living things into three different kingdoms. In the United States, many scientists now identify three domains, or groups. Some still use the five different kingdoms of living things. They are: Animalia, Plantae, Fungi, Protista, and Bacteria (and sometimes Archaea). These kingdoms were then divided into phyla, which described a basic structure of a living thing. For example, worms and birds belong to different phyla because their bodies are designed differently. From there, living things were divided into smaller groupings, first by class, then by order, family, genus, and species. All of these categories describe physical characteristics, such as whether an animal is warm- or cold-blooded, and whether it has an internal spine to support its body, or a crunchy outer shell called an **exoskeleton**.

The common housefly belongs to the *Brachycera* **suborder. It is a member of the** *Muscidae* **family,** *Musca* **genus, and** *domestica* **species. So,** *Musca domestica* **is a fancy way of saying housefly.**

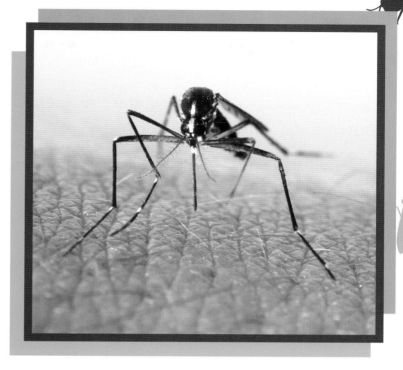

Diptera, **or true flies, belong to a huge order that includes mosquitoes, gnats, midges, and hundreds of different flies. Mosquitoes belong to the** *Nematocera* **suborder.**

Anatomy Lesson

Flies have hard exoskeletons made of chitin, a tough material that is a little bit like fingernails. The chitin protects the fly's body when it crashes into a window, and it prevents the fly from getting waterlogged when it lands in a puddle. Hundreds of tiny hairs on the fly's body allow it to sense the smallest changes in the air around it. A fly can sense a swatter moving toward it, or a sugary bowl of fruit sitting on a table several feet away.

Unlike humans, flies have greenish-yellow blood.

CRAWLY FACT

Tube Feeders

Flies have long feeding tubes with spongy tips at the end, which soak up liquidy foods. Powerful pumps inside their heads help them suck. Flies do not have stomachs, but three different guts that allow them to break down food. The foregut has a special gland that **secretes** saliva and vomit to help liquefy food. The midgut is where food is digested so that nutrients can be carried to different parts of the fly's body. The hindgut is the fly's waste tank. Food that is not needed is passed out of its body through the hindgut. When the fly overeats, food immediately bypasses digestion and heads straight for the hindgut, where it is excreted. The fly must do this to keep light for flying.

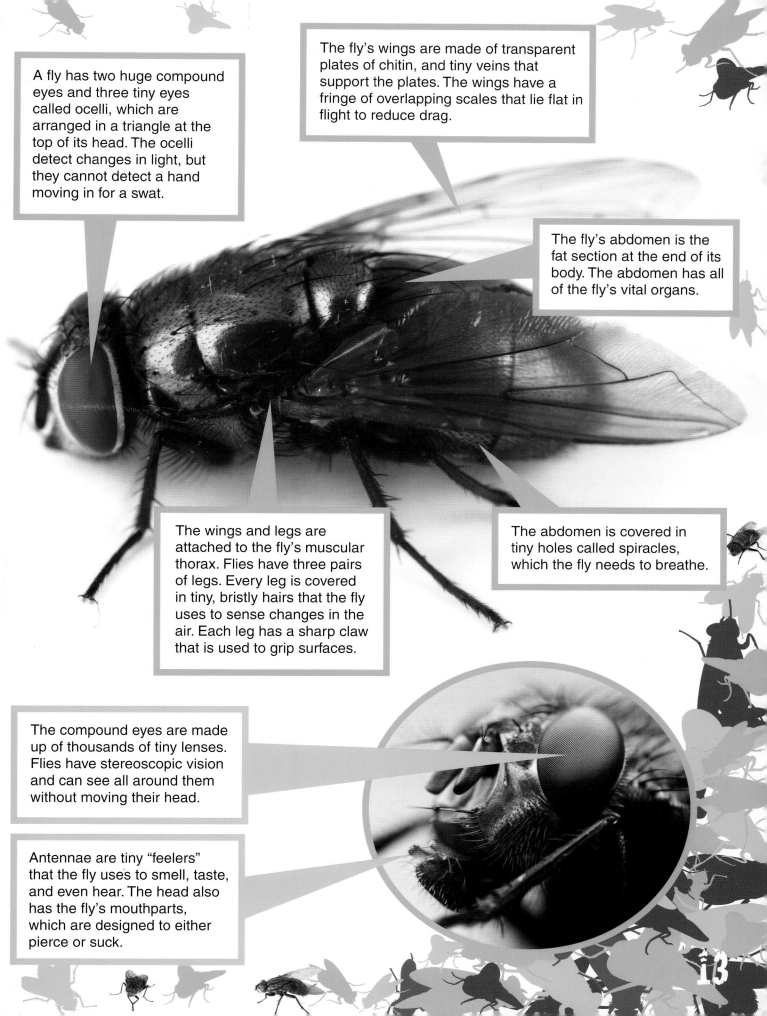

A fly has two huge compound eyes and three tiny eyes called ocelli, which are arranged in a triangle at the top of its head. The ocelli detect changes in light, but they cannot detect a hand moving in for a swat.

The fly's wings are made of transparent plates of chitin, and tiny veins that support the plates. The wings have a fringe of overlapping scales that lie flat in flight to reduce drag.

The fly's abdomen is the fat section at the end of its body. The abdomen has all of the fly's vital organs.

The wings and legs are attached to the fly's muscular thorax. Flies have three pairs of legs. Every leg is covered in tiny, bristly hairs that the fly uses to sense changes in the air. Each leg has a sharp claw that is used to grip surfaces.

The abdomen is covered in tiny holes called spiracles, which the fly needs to breathe.

The compound eyes are made up of thousands of tiny lenses. Flies have stereoscopic vision and can see all around them without moving their head.

Antennae are tiny "feelers" that the fly uses to smell, taste, and even hear. The head also has the fly's mouthparts, which are designed to either pierce or suck.

13

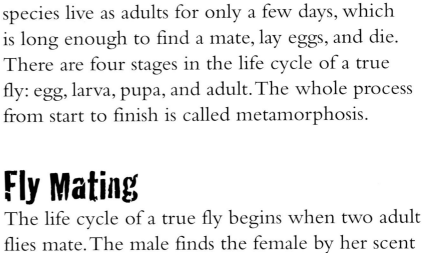

Cycle of Life

The life cycle of true flies is very short. Some species live as adults for only a few days, which is long enough to find a mate, lay eggs, and die. There are four stages in the life cycle of a true fly: egg, larva, pupa, and adult. The whole process from start to finish is called metamorphosis.

Fly Mating

The life cycle of a true fly begins when two adult flies mate. The male finds the female by her scent and wing beat. Once they mate, the female looks for sources of protein that will help her eggs develop, and a warm, moist place to lay her eggs. Rotting fruit, meat, or decaying road kill are perfect places for egg laying.

Larva Life

A day or two later, the eggs hatch into tiny white worms called larvae, or maggots. They have thin, slimy bodies and mouth hooks for eating. And do they ever eat! Flies eat as much as they can as maggots, because it is the only time that they can grow before they have hard exoskeletons as adults. Larvae eat for about a week, until they triple in size, molting, or shedding their skin as they outgrow it. Most larvae molt three times before they become pupae.

After mating, the female lays her eggs where they can safely become larvae.

Housefly Life Cycle

A housefly's life cycle is nine to 25 days from start to finish.

Flies that feed on blood, such as horseflies, take from 23-25 days to mature from egg to adult.

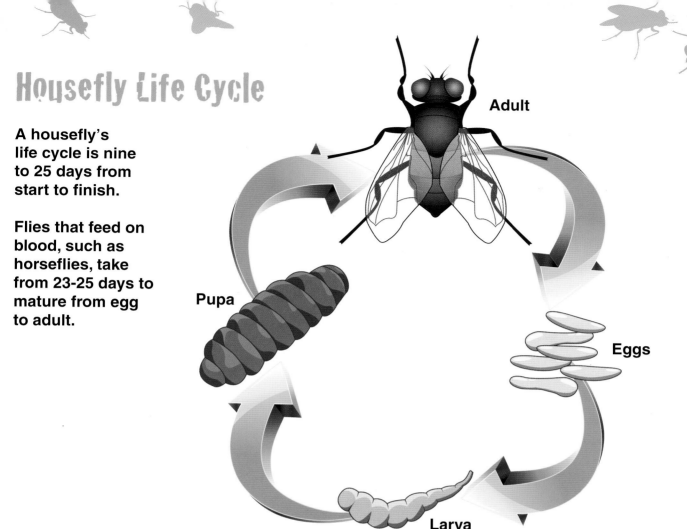

Adult

Pupa

Eggs

Larva

Larva to Fly

Once the larvae have eaten as much as they can, they crawl to a dry, safe place to become pupae. Their skin dries into a hard casing. From the outside, it looks like nothing is happening, but inside the pupa, big changes are taking place. At this stage, flies build all of their adult body parts. They also develop muscles and nerves. Flies stay in the pupae stage from five or six days to one month, depending on the temperature. Warmer weather speeds up the process. When flies are fully formed, the casing cracks open. Adult flies rest for a few minutes, holding their wings out to dry. When dry, the flies take to the air. Adult flies live from 20 to 30 days, depending on whether or not a swatter cuts their life short. Female flies are ready to mate about 36 hours after emerging from their pupae casings.

Maggotville

Maggots are the creepy, crawling worms that devour spoiled food and eat that squirrel carcass at the side of the road. Most people are completely grossed out by maggots, but these wannabe flies play an important role in several food chains.

Life of a Maggot

The first thing a maggot does after it hatches is eat its own casing, which is packed with nutrients that the maggot needs to kick-start a major growth spurt. Maggots are different sizes, depending on the species. Most fly maggots are less than a quarter of an inch (6 millimeters) long, but they do not stay that size. Maggots triple in size before they turn into pupae, molting their skin three times as they grow.

Even food regulators know that maggots are an inescapable fact of life. In the United States, the Food and Drug Administration (FDA) says that 40 maggots per can of mushrooms or corn will not pose a hazard to your health.

What does a maggot eat? Everything and anything! They snag food with sharp little mouth hooks that protrude from their heads.

Looks like macaroni but tastes like...maggots! Fly maggots make excellent fish bait.

Nature's Little Helpers

Maggots seem like filthy creatures, but the truth is that the world would be a lot dirtier without them. Maggots break down decomposing matter such as animal carcasses. They work their way through garbage dumps, and keep compost heaps from spilling over with rotten gunk. Maggots are also bred for fishing bait and fed to pet reptiles, such as lizards and snakes, as well as pet birds.

THAT'S CREEPY

Maggoty Science

Maggots can be very helpful to forensic scientists, who study dead bodies to learn more about how and why people die. The presence of flies on a body usually means that a person has not been dead very long. Maggots indicate that the person has been dead for a few days to a few weeks. Gross fact: maggots eat the face of a body first because they like wet places, like eye sockets, nose cavities, mouths, and ear holes.

19

Infestation!

Flies love to be with people. They inhabit drains, garbage cans, litter boxes, and refrigerators. Usually, they are only noticed when they become adults, but fly eggs, maggots, and pupae can be found just about anywhere. But how many flies are too many?

What is it?

An infestation is a big word for a simple situation: too many flies! A cloud of flies hanging out by the garbage can, or a clump of maggots eating a piece of meat stuck in the kitchen drain is an infestation. Flies lay their eggs by the hundreds, so one day of hatching can turn a home into a crawling, buzzing nightmare. In other words, it can take only a single fly to create an infestation.

Flies are ectothermic, which means they cannot generate their own body heat. That is why they are attracted to warm things and gather under porch lights after the sun has set.

Getting Rid of Flies

The best way to keep a home fly-free is to get rid of their favorite breeding places. It is a good idea to have tight-fitting lids over garbage cans, and to take out the garbage every day. Keep fruit in the fridge rather than in a bowl, especially on warm summer days. Most homes have windows with screens, but it is wise to check them regularly for holes. It is also important to cover the compost heap, and to make sure it is located as far from the house as possible.

The cattle and trash at this dumpsite are heaven for a fly!

CRAWLY FACT

Squatter's Rights

If one fruit fly makes it inside, it will quickly find a fruit bowl, or a banana peel in the garbage to lay its eggs in. The next day, hundreds of tiny, hungry fruit flies will swarm the bowl, looking for mates and a place to lay their eggs. The reason why fruit flies take over so quickly is that they lay hundreds of eggs, and the eggs hatch within 24 hours. The larvae are so tiny that they can be hard to see, so they become adults before anyone notices the maggots.

Fruit flies love rotting fruit.

Bloodsuckers

Bloodsuckers

Not all flies bite, but watch out for the ones that do! Some of the true flies that suck the blood of humans and animals are mosquitoes, black flies, horseflies, tiny midges, tsetse flies, and deerflies. The bites that they leave behind can swell into painful, itchy welts. Bloodsucking flies can also spread deadly diseases.

Feeding Frenzy

How do they do it? Bloodsuckers use their keen senses to find their victims. They are attracted to the carbon dioxide in exhaled breath, as well as salty sweat on the skin. Once the bloodsucker has landed, it dives in with its mouthparts and cuts the skin to suck up its meal. To make the blood flow faster, bloodsuckers inject saliva that contains an **anticoagulant**, which prevents the blood from clotting. Soft membranes between the insect's body segments stretch, allowing its abdomen to expand as it fills with blood.

Which way is up? Horse flies are named for their love of horses. These horses are wearing protective gear to prevent the brutal bloodsuckers from biting.

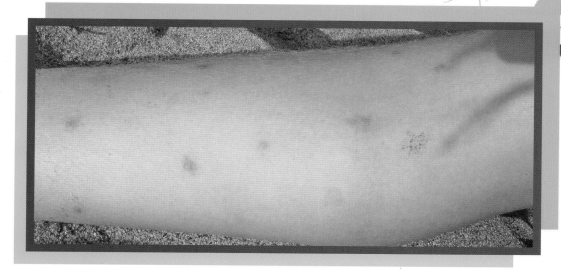

Mosquitoes are relentless feeders, leaving behind red, itchy welts on their victims.

Spreading Disease

Some biting flies are more than just annoying. They spread diseases in humans and animals. Mosquitoes are the most well known biters. Their sharp proboscises are like dirty needles. If they feed on a disease-ridden animal, they can pass the infection onto the next animal or person they bite. That is because a small amount of blood remains in their proboscises after feeding. When they pierce the next person, a very tiny amount of blood can be injected when they puncture the skin for their next meal. Moquitoes can spread some nasty diseases including malaria and West Nile virus. Deerflies and horseflies are vicious biters. They can spread bartonellosis, which causes trench fever and cat scratch fever.

A nature photographer wears protective netting and clothing to prevent mosquito and fly bites.

Flies have many enemies that threaten their lives. Humans are one of their biggest predators, who arm themselves with flyswatters, rolled up newspapers, and **insecticides**. It is amazing that flies survive at all!

Fly Predators

Flies fall victim to many different predators. Frogs, birds, dragonflies, and bats love to eat flies. Spiders catch flies in their webs. The fine strands are hard for flies to see, so they can easily become stuck in these sticky webs. The spider bites the helpless fly with its fangs and poisons it with venom. This paralyzes the fly, allowing the spider to wrap the fly in a silky cocoon and save it for later. But it is not just adult flies that get eaten alive. Fish and hungry insects dine on fly larvae. One of the most efficient fly killers is a fungus called Empusa muscae. This silent exterminator appears as white spots on a fly's body, and it slowly eats at the fly until there is nothing left of it.

Hungry bats can eat up to 1,000 mosquitoes in one hour.

Gotcha! Spiders catch and eat flies.

Like bees, flies are important pollinators. Flies become dusted in pollen when they feed on the nectar of flowers. When they move to another flower, they leave pollen residue behind, fertilizing the flower so it can produce seeds.

Fly Prey

Each fly species has a different diet and way of eating. Parasitic flies, such as tachinid flies, live inside other animals at the larval stage, usually killing their host before they become adults. Bloodsucking flies are not picky about their food, as long as it is blood. That means they are happy drinking from a bird, human, or horse. Non-parasitic flies eat rotten fruit and the nectar of flowers.

Dining Out

Some flies have very interesting eating habits. Robber flies, sometimes called assassin flies, eat their prey from the inside out. They are very quick, and can catch prey in mid-flight with their strong, gripping legs. They use their proboscis to dig into their victim's body and suck their guts into their mouths. Then they discard their victim's husk and fly away. Bees and spiders are favorite meals of the robber fly.

Bee flies have hairy, yellow-and-black striped bodies. They look so much like real bees that they can creep up to a beehive and lay their eggs close to the entrance of the hive. When the eggs hatch, the larvae crawl into the beehive, looking for food. They eat bee larvae and pupae.

Shoo Fly!

People have been trying to get rid of flies for centuries. Swatting them is a classic way to kill them, but since flies have exceptional vision, they can be hard to hit. Swatting can be an **unsanitary** way of killing flies, as their guts and bacteria-laden body parts will get all over the swatter, shoe, magazine, hand, or whatever else is used to squash them. Gross!

Gotcha!

Trapping flies is a more sanitary way of dealing with them. Light traps use ultraviolet light to attract and trap flies. Humans cannot see ultraviolet light, but flies love it. They fly toward the light and into a box that prevents them from getting out. Ultraviolet light traps are good for fighting flies indoors because they can be mounted to walls and doors. Flypaper is a sticky strip that can be taped to walls. The problem with flypaper is that flies are not naturally attracted to it, so the flies have to fly very close to the sticky strips to get stuck. Flypaper is also unsanitary as they become covered in flies.

Flyswatters are a low-tech way of getting rid of flies.

Chemical Arsenal

Insect sprays that contain DEET can be applied to the skin. When a fly or mosquito lands on the skin, the chemicals in the spray harm the fly's body. The chemicals stop the fly's muscles from contracting, making it unable to fly. Other chemicals block the fly's spiracles so that it cannot breathe.

Flypaper is a type of sticky-coated paper. Once flies touch the paper, they are stuck to it for good.

Home Remedies

There are some interesting ways to get rid of flies that don't involve zapping, squashing, or spraying them. One solution is using homemade fly traps made with empty glass jars. Put a little bit of jam or jelly into a jar, and add some water. Next, stab some holes in the lid with a screwdriver, and screw the lid back onto the jar. Flies will be attracted to the sweet jam, and fly into the jar through the holes. Once inside, they won't be able to find a spot to land that is not sticky, and will become trapped in the jar.

A Venus fly trap, is a carnivorous, or flesh eating, plant. When flies and other insects come close to the plants leaves, sensitive prickly hairs on the plant are stimulated, making the leaf snap shut.

Fly Fascination

Flies have been on the planet longer than humans. So, it is not surprising that flies have flown into popular culture, movies, songs, recipes, and common expressions.

FLIES ON FILM

In 1958, *The Fly* horrified and delighted science fiction fans. The movie, based on a short story by George Langelaan, is about a strange scientist who is obsessed with time travel. He creates a device that can teleport objects, or move objects from one place or space in time to another, with the press of a button. When a fly crawls into the scientist's device, something goes wrong and causes the scientist to turn into a fly. The movie was a huge success, and was followed by two sequels, *Return of the Fly*, and *Curse of the Fly*. The original movie was remade in 1986.

BOOKWORMS

Flies have appeared in literature for centuries. "Little Fly," written by English poet William Blake asks: "Am not I / A fly like thee? / Or art not thou / A man like me?" These questions show that the poet feels his life is small and insignificant, like a tiny fly. The children's song, "I Know An Old Lady Who Swallowed A Fly" is about a woman who becomes so uncomfortable that she swallows a spider to catch the fly. She then swallows a bird to catch the spider, and larger animals after that until she finally dies.

Shoo-fly pie is a traditional dessert of the Pennsylvania Dutch. The pie has a sweet molasses filling, which attracts flies that need to be "shooed."

ON THE WALL

Flies are such a big part of our lives that they have even found a way into common expressions. Ever hear the phrase: "I'd like to be a fly on the wall"? The meaning of this expression is that flies on the wall see and hear all that we do, so wanting to be a fly on the wall is a way of saying that a person would like to be a silent bystander to an event or conversation that took place. This clever expression suggests that people and flies are inseparable in their existence. A "fly in the ointment" is an expression to describe a small flaw that ruins something.

A fly on the wall (or table) in this room would be able to hear the conversation and be unnoticed.

That's So Fly!

Flies are amazing! They are considered both an annoyance and a help to humans. There is so much you can learn from flies. Some entomologists spend their whole working lives studying just a few kinds of flies. Other scientists have used fly behavior as a model to create robotic flies that will eventually be used as spy cameras or to locate bombs and chemicals used in warfare. Want to know more interesting facts about flies? Read on:

When light refracts off the compound eyes of a horsefly, it can make a miniature rainbow.

In some parts of the world, people eat maggots by choice! In Germany, people line up around the block to taste one restaurant's famous maggot ice cream. In Italy, people eat casu marzu, a special cheese made from sheep's milk. Maggots are allowed to wriggle through the cheese while it is hardening, giving it an extra creamy texture and tangy flavor. The maggots are usually taken out before it is sold in markets, but some people prefer to eat it maggots and all!

A few species of flies and mosquitoes thrive in the icy Arctic. They survive by sitting in white cup-shaped flowers that attract the sun and retain heat.

Flies do not have eyelids. They use their hairy legs to scrape over the surface of their eyes for optimal eyesight.

The Kutzadika'a are a Native American people who lived in central California. In the summer months, they came to the Mono Lake Basin area on the east coast. The lake was home to alkali flies, which the Kutzadika'a collected from shallow pools of Mono Lake, to be dried and eaten. The flies are very high in fat and protein, and were a delicacy to the Kutzadika'a, who traded it to other groups of people. Alkali flies still swarm Mono Lake today.

California's Mono Lake, home to the Alkali fly

Flies have brains inside their heads, as well as miniature nerve centers all over their body, which control different functions such as breathing, walking, and flying. For that reason, flies can lose their heads and continue to fly, walk, and lay eggs.

The first effort to build the Panama Canal, the link between the Pacific Ocean and the Caribbean Sea, was abandoned in 1893. The reason? About 20,000 workers died from the mosquito-spread diseases malaria and yellow fever.

Pest Detective

Flies are everywhere—in your back yard, at the park, and inside your house. You can learn a lot about them by studying them firsthand. The next time a fly invades your home, watch it closely. Does is seem to rub its feet together? How does it fly? What is it attracted to and where does it land? Check out the following resources to learn more about where to find flies, how to catch them, and ways to classify them.

WEB SITES

Here are some cool sites to check out:

Pestworld for Kids
www.pestworldforkids.org/flies.html
This is a great site for learning about insects of all kinds. Find pictures, read information sheets, get homework help, and play games. You can also learn fun science experiments that you can do at home.

Insects.org
www.insects.org/
This Web site provides in-depth "Bug Bios," or information on many different kinds of insects, including flies and mosquitoes. Cool graphics and bite-sized bits of information make it easy to learn.

Smithsonian Institution: BugInfo
www.si.edu/Encyclopedia_SI/nmnh/buginfo/start.htm
Look up different types of bugs and insects, and research special topics such as insect flight, pheromones, and bug hibernation. A list of science fair projects help you learn more and have fun.

Earthlife: Wonderful World of Insects
www.earthlife.net/insects/six.html
Search the index of topics for special information on *Diptera* flies. Links to clubs for insect lovers and book reviews are also available.

KidInfo: Insects
www.kidinfo.com/Science/insects.html
This site is a great place to start research. It provides links and descriptions of other useful sites on insects, as well as photos and videos.

Here are some great books on flies, mosquitoes, and other insects:

The Insecto-Files, by Helaine Becker.
Toronto: Maple Tree Press, 2009.

Focus on Flies, by Norma Dixon.
Markham: Fitzhenry & Whiteside, 2008.

The Housefly, by Heiderose and Andreas Fischer-Nagel.
Minneapolis: Carolrhoda Books, 1990.

Fly, by Karen Harley, Chris Macro, and Philip Taylor.
Chicago: Reed Educational, 2000.

The Secret World of Flies, by John Woodward.
Chicago: Raintree, 2004

**Want to see flies up close and personal?
Here are some great places to visit:**

American Museum of Natural History
Central Park West at 79th Street
New York, NY 10024-5192
Phone: (212) 769-5100

The Insect Zoo at San Francisco Zoo
1 Zoo Road
San Francisco, CA 94132
Phone: (415) 753-7080

Invertebrate Exhibit, The National Zoo
3001 Connecticut Ave., NW
Washington, DC 20008
Phone: (540) 635-6500

**The O. Orkin Insect Zoo at the National
Museum of Natural History, Smithsonian**
10th Street and Constitution Ave., NW
Washington, DC 20560
Phone: (202) 633-1000

Glossary

adapting To change or adjust to a new environment or condition

amber The fossilized resin of a prehistoric tree that sometimes contains the remains of insects

American Civil War A war between the northern states (the Union) and the southern states (the Confederacy) that took place from 1861–1865

amputation To cut off a limb

anticoagulant A substance that causes blood to flow freely

bacteria Microorganisms that can cause disease that are sometimes spread through flies or other insects

carbon dioxide Colorless and odorless gas that is naturally present in air

class A category or grouping of things

compound eyes Eyes that consist of a number of small visual units

decaying Rotting or decomposing naturally

DEET A chemical insect repellent

defecate To discharge waste, or poop

entomologist A scientist, or zoologist who studies insects

exoskeleton A hard outer covering for some insects that provides support and protection

feces Waste matter, or poop

fertilize To cause an egg to develop into a new life after mating

insecticides A substance, sometimes chemical, used for killing insects

maggot The soft, legless larva of a fly

New World North and South America

parasite An organism that lives on or in another organism, called a host

secretes To produce and discharge a substance from the body

species A group of living organisms that are similar to one another

taxonomy A scientific method of classifying something, particularly living things

typhoid An infectious fever caused by a bacteria spread by some insects when they bite

unsanitary Something that is unhealthy, germ-ridden, or unclean

Index